Reycraft Books
55 Fifth Avenue
New York, NY 10003
Reycraftbooks.com

In memory of Gramma Erle—A.W.

Library of Congress Control Number: 2020908313

ISBN: 978-1-4788-6962-7

Photograph credits: Jacket Front, Jacket Back, Front Cover, Back Cover: Kletr/Shutterstock; Jacket Spine, Book Spine, Page 12F: LordRunar/Getty Images; Front Flap: Butterfly Hunter/Shutterstock; Inside Front Flap, Page 16A: MediaProduction/Getty Images; Inside Front Jacket A: Freder/Getty Images; Inside Front Jacket B: April30/Getty Images; Inside Back Jacket A: ACormier/Getty Images; Inside Back Jacket B: Phant/Shutterstock; Inside Back Flap: AB Photographie/Shutterstock; Back Flap, Page 32B: Courtesy of Phung Luu; Poster A: Sandra Conner/Alamy; Poster B, Pages 19B, 29B: Arterra/Getty Images; Poster C: Patrick Rolands/Shutterstock; Poster D, Page 29C: wwing/Getty Images; Poster E, Pages 6A, 29D: Buiten-Beeld/Alamy; Poster F, Page 28C: Floridapfe from S.Korea Kim in cherl/Getty Images; Title Page, Pages 3F, K: GlobalP/Getty Images; Page 2: Daniel J Nevares/Getty Images; Page 3A: Stephen Lavery/Shutterstock; Page 3B: Ian Dyball/Getty Images; Page 3C: Dagmara Ksandrova/Shutterstock; Page 3D: GoWildPhotography/Shutterstock; Page 3E: wWeiss Lichtspiele/Getty Images; Page 3G: stevegeer/Getty Images; Page 3H: J R Price/Shutterstock; Page 3I: MattCuda/Getty Images; Page 3J: Svetlana Turchenick/Shutterstock; Page 3L: vizland/Getty Images; Page 4: Brad Leue/Alamy; Page 5A: Charles Melton/Alamy; Page 5B: agefotostock/Alamy; Page 5C: Ghost Bear/Shutterstock; Page 6B: pchoui/Getty Images; Page 6C: Noella Ballenger/Alamy; Page 6D: jimkruger/Getty Images; Pages 6E, 7: tatianaput/Getty Images; Page 8: michaklootwijk/Getty Images; Page 9A: Jim Cumming/Shutterstock; Pages 9B, 30B: Sabena Jane Blackbird/Alamy; Pages 10A, 11A: holwichaikawee/Getty Images; Page 10B: RHJ/Getty Images; Page 11B: Petr Simon/Shutterstock; Page 11C: Rafael Martos Martins/Shutterstock; Page 11D: Chris Wallace/Alamy; Page 11E: Marc_Latremouille/Getty Images; Pages 12A, 13A: jaroslava V/Shutterstock; Page 12B: Miro Vrlik Photography/Shutterstock; Page 12C: Kaphoto/Getty Images; Page 12D: Baranov E/Shutterstock; Page 12E: Leena Robinson/Shutterstock; Page 12G: Zocha_K/Getty Images; Page 12H: Sharath V Jois/Getty Images; Page 13B: DavidMednick/Getty Images; Page 14: mlorenzphotography/Getty Images; Page 15A: chriszwaenepoel/Getty Images; Page 15B: Montipaiton/Shutterstock; Page 15C: aaltair/Shutterstock; Page 15D: Ian_Sherriffs/Getty Images; Page 15E: Malcolm Brice/Alamy; Page 15F: Holger Kirk/Shutterstock; Page 15G: allanw/Shutterstock; Page 15H: Jillian Cooper/Getty Images; Page 15I: georgesanker.com/Alamy; Pages 15J–L: makasana photo/Alamy; Page 16B: JillLang/Getty Images; Page 16C: gemredding/Getty Images; Page 17A: Noorhussain/Getty Images; Page 17B: Michael Morse/Getty Images; Page 18A: LesPalenik/Shutterstock; Page 18B: Michael Shake/Shutterstock; Page 18C: esvetleishaya/Getty Images; Page 19A, 28A: kiszon pascal/Getty Images; Page 20A: mg7/Getty Images; Page 20B: Philip Mugridge/Alamy; Page 20C: Nature Photographers Ltd/Alamy; Pages 20D, 21: Voodison328/Shutterstock; Page 22A: Weber/Getty Images; Pages 22B, 23A: Erhard Nerger/Getty Images; Page 22C: Tobyphotos/Shutterstock; Page 22D: 101cats/Getty Images; Page 23B: Albert Beukhof/Shutterstock; Pages 24, 25A: All Canada Photos/Alamy; Page 25B: Sandy Scott/500px/Getty Images; Page 26A: Ann and Steve Toon/Alamy; Pages 26B, 27: Woofit/Shutterstock; Page 28B: bjorn999/Getty Images; Pages 28D, 29A: Samantha Nicol Art Photography/Getty Images; Pages 30A, 31: CHROMORANGE/Martin Schroder/Alamy; Pages 30C, D: Big Foot Productions/Shutterstock; Page 30E: Dorling Kindersley ltd/Alamy; Page 30F: By Ian Miles-Flashpoint Pictures/Alamy; Page 30G: stockphotofan1/Shutterstock; Page 32A: Dorling Kindersley/Getty Images

Illustration credits: Page 3, 5b, 7, 9b, 11, 13b, 15, 17, 19, 21, 23, 25: JuanbJuan Oliver; Page 5a, 8, 9a, 13a: Franco Rivolli

Printed in Dongguan, China. 8557/0721/18095

10 9 8 7 6 5 4 3 2

First Edition Hardcover published by Reycraft Books

Reycraft Books and Newmark Learning, LLC. support diversity and the First Amendment, and celebrate the right to read.

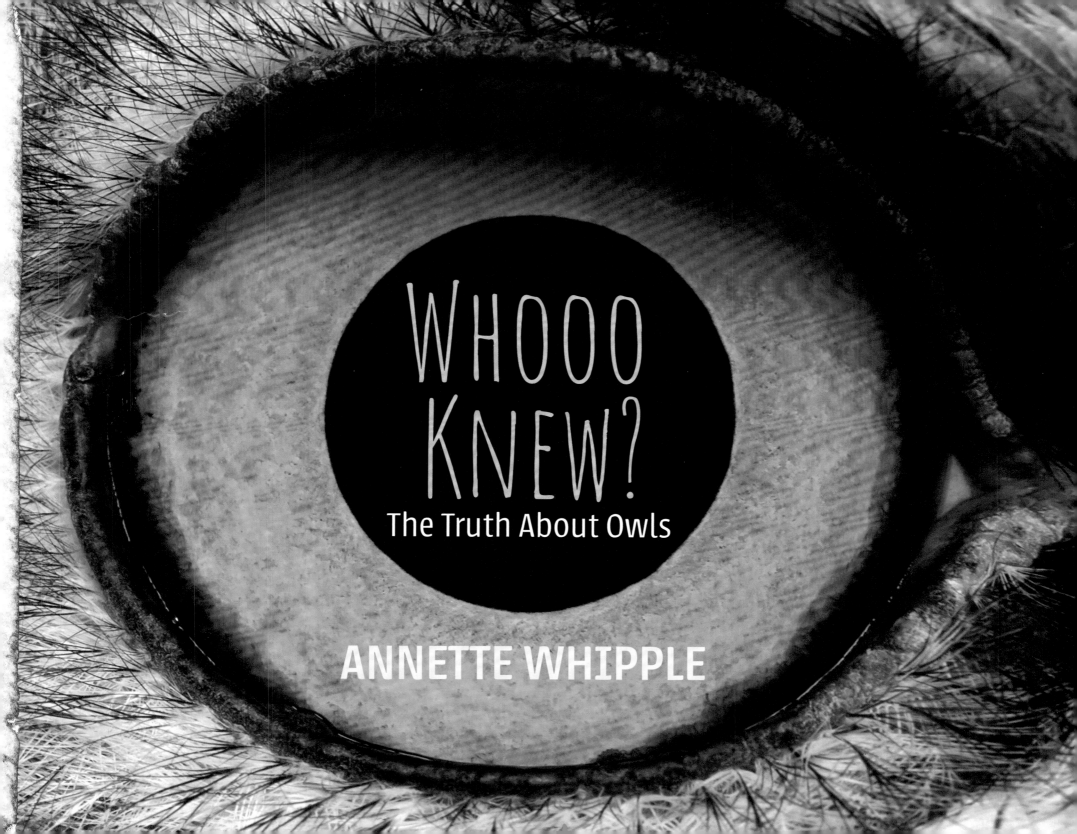

WHOOO KNEW?

The Truth About Owls

ANNETTE WHIPPLE

WHOOO'S THERE?

THE UNFORGETTABLE CALL.

THE GLOWING EYES.

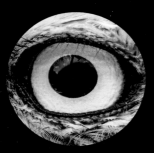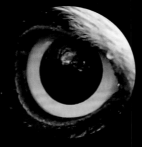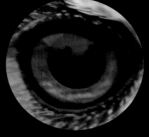

THE FIERCE BEAK.

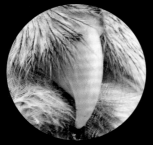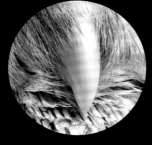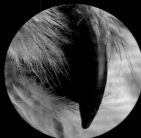

You recognize an owl when you hear or see one,
but do you really know these birds?

Whooo Knew?

Did you think
owls just hoot?
NAH.

We make lots of sounds. Listen for
screeches, whistles, trills, and even barks.
You can know our species by our sounds.
I don't want you to see me, but you may
hear me near a forest. Other owls live in
deserts, rainforests, and the tundra. We're
"owl" over the world—even in cities.

3

WHAT'S

Whooo
Knew?

4

FOR DINNER?

Elf Owl

As predators, owls survive by hunting other animals, often small mammals like rats. Owls choose their meals based on their species.

Short-eared Owl

The Elf Owl is the smallest owl. It weighs as much as a hard-boiled egg and is as tall as a soda can. It typically satisfies its appetite with insects. The medium-sized Short-eared Owl eats small birds and rodents like voles. But the Great Horned Owl—the ruler of North America's skies—feasts on opossums, geese, and skunks. It even eats smaller owls.

Great Horned Owl

Don't hate me just because I eat other owls.

Sometimes dinner must be whatever—or whoooever—I can find. I gobble up plenty of rodents you call pests.

5

How Do Owls Hunt?

She waits.   She watches.   She listens.

6

The owl hears a mouse scurry across a nearby field. She flies silently through the sky, targeted on her prey.

She dives. She spreads her talons.

SNATCH!

The owl carries it away.

The attack surprises my prey as my talons capture and squeeze it. I swallow my dinner whole—and alive. My powerful beak rips larger meals like rabbits into gulp-size pieces.

7

DO OWLS PUKE?

The owl hunts a mouse.

The owl eats the mouse.

The owl digests the mouse.

The owl spits up a pellet.

The owl returns to the perch with a mouse in her beak. She tosses and then gulps down the entire mouse—headfirst.

The first part of the owl's stomach coats the mouse in digestive juices. Then the food moves to another part of the stomach. The bones, fur, and teeth can't be digested, so they're packed into a tight pellet. After about ten hours the owl regurgitates, or coughs out, the pellet. Now the owl can eat again.

Bone Sorting Charts

	BIRDS	MOLES	RODENTS
SKULLS			
JAWS			
SHOULDER BLADES			
FRONT LEGS			
HIPS			
HIND LEGS			

Whooo Knew?

Whooo puked? It wasn't me. I wasn't sick. I regurgitated the pellet, with a bit of a cough. If you're the curious type, look inside my pellet to learn what I had for dinner. That's if you're *really curious.*

Do Owls Sleep

Barn Owl

During the day, most owls nap and hide in their roost. They're active at night. But not all owls are nocturnal.

ALL DAY?

Burrowing Owl

Some owls are active at dawn and dusk. Burrowing Owls hunt around sunrise and sunset, so they rest during the day and night.

Northern Hawk Owl

Northern Hawk Owls are different from most owls. They spend their days awake and hunting. They nap at night.

Whooo Knew?

I'm a Snowy Owl.

Summer days in the arctic are long, so I find plenty of small mammals like lemmings while the sun shines. I even hunt birds and fish. Owls must be aware of danger, so we don't sleep deeply.

Instead, we nap whenever we can.

11

Do Owls See in the Dark?

A truck's headlights shine on an owl.
He doesn't squint. He doesn't even blink.
His eyes are designed to see with or without light.

When lights shine on an owl, the dark center of his eyes—the pupils—instantly shrink. In the dark, eyes need more light to see, so the pupil gets bigger.

Even the shape of the owl's eyes help him to see in the dark. The eyes are like long tubes, not balls. The tubes give extra space for rod cells that help the owl see shapes and movement in low light.

Whooo Knew?

My farsighted vision helps me hunt, but I can't see well up close. I don't need glasses. I use my whiskers to "see" my food before I devour it.

Gulp!

Can Owls Spin Their Heads Around?

White-faced Scops Owl

14

Long-eared Owl

Barn Owl

White-faced Scops Owl

Great Gray Owl

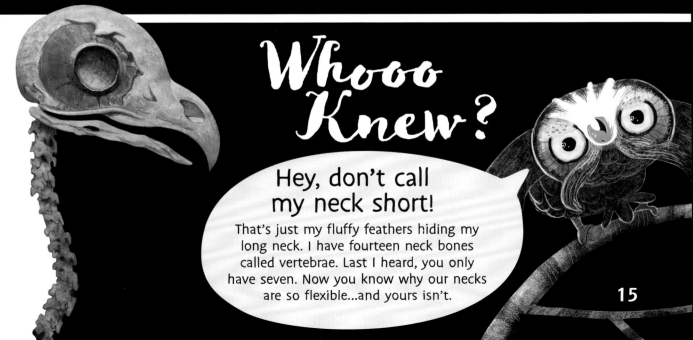

Owls' eyes never move. They just look straight ahead. Since owls' eyes don't look around, owls move their heads up, down, and all around to see.

Owls have extra neck bones. That's why they're super flexible. They almost rotate, or turn, their heads completely upside down. And they almost turn it in a full circle.

Whooo Knew?

Hey, don't call my neck short!

That's just my fluffy feathers hiding my long neck. I have fourteen neck bones called vertebrae. Last I heard, you only have seven. Now you know why our necks are so flexible...and yours isn't.

15

What Good Are FEATHERS?

Feathers cover owls' bodies. Each kind of owl has its own color and pattern to help it hide. It's called camouflage, and it helps owls blend in with their surroundings.

Like all birds, feathers help owls fly. But the feathers of owls are different from other birds. Most owls fly without a sound because of their soft and jagged wing feathers.

16

Pallid Scops Owl

Great Horned Owl

Whooo Knew?

Hee hee!

Did I scare you? We puff up our feathers when we're spooked. Don't get too close because we like to keep some secrets. Scientists don't know everything about us—yet.

17

What Good Are Ear Tufts?

Some owls have ear tufts on top of their heads. But those aren't ears at all. They're just feathers. Owls show their mood with ear tufts. A watchful owl keeps his ear tufts raised. An irritated owl lays them flat. Male and female owls even communicate with ear tufts during courtship.

Owls' actual ears are on the sides of their heads. These openings hide under feathers. They hear the softest of sounds—like a mouse's footsteps. Once an owl locates a sound, she knows where to find her prey.

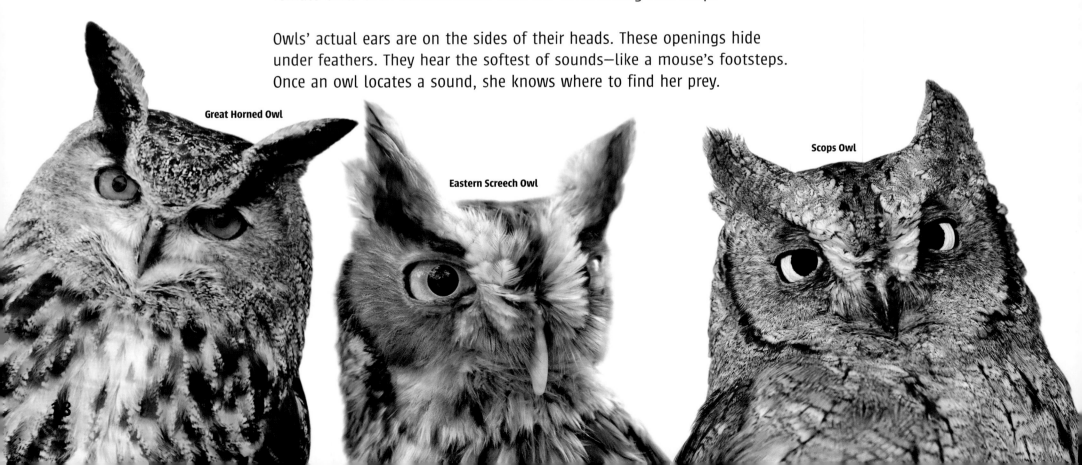

Great Horned Owl

Eastern Screech Owl

Scops Owl

Barred Eagle Owl

Whooo Knew?

All owls have incredible hearing, but my Barn Owl friends have unusually large ear structures and exceptional hearing. Many of us have one ear higher than the other, which helps us to target our prey.

Then...dinnertime!

WHAT'S AN OWL NEST LIKE?

Snowy Owl

Barn Owl

Elf Owl

Owls don't build nests. So, what do they do? Most use sheltered holes made by woodpeckers or formed when a branch breaks. Some large owls use stick nests from other birds, like herons or hawks. Other owls live in cracks in rocks or even the sides of a building.

Barn owls live near people and make their homes in church towers, barns, and warehouses.

The Snowy Owl doesn't find a hole, a crack, or an old nest. The female lays eggs on the ground of the treeless tundra.

Burrowing Owl

Whooo Knew?

Ah, home sweet home.
Few predators try to get past the spines of this giant cactus where Elf Owls live. It even keeps the family cool in the desert sun.

WHAT DO OWL BABIES DO?

A mother owl feeds her young owlets small scraps of food.

The owlets grow. Feathers replace the fluffy white down covering the owlets. Soon they walk and climb.

The owlets spread out and hide on branches near the nest.

SQUEAK. SQUEAK. SQUEAK.

POUNCE!

An owlet grabs its first prey. It's a beetle.

Once mature, owls find territories of their own. They hunt small animals and typically pair off with a mate in the winter.

Whooo Knew?

My mama laid eggs over many days, so we hatched at different times. But don't worry about me. As the oldest, I make sure I get more food than anyone else. My siblings might think I'm greedy, but if anyone goes hungry, it won't be me.

23

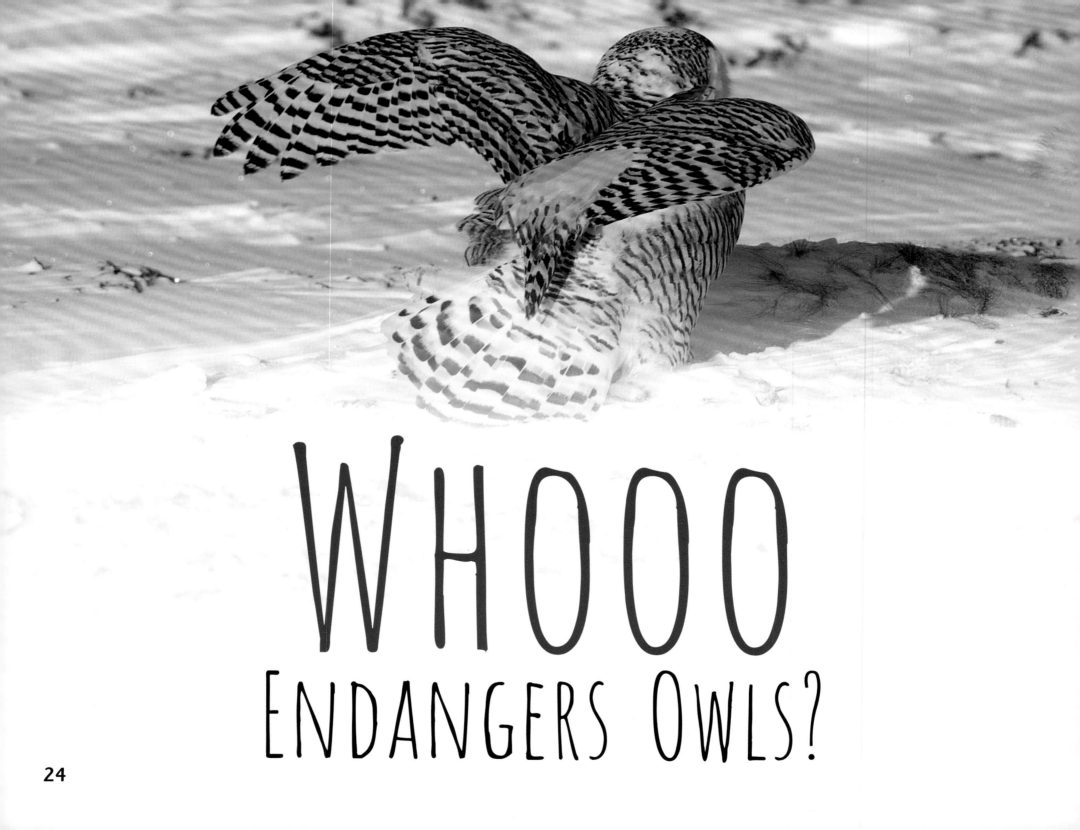

WHOOO
ENDANGERS OWLS?

Eagle Owl

Many owlets don't live through their first year of life. Disease and starvation put young owls in danger. Predators threaten owls, too. Animals like raccoons and foxes often prey on owl eggs and owlets. Larger owls and hawks also hunt owls—even adult owls.

Some people hurt owls. Vehicles and owls collide along busy highways.

Yet many owlets grow up with ...

THE UNFORGETTABLE CALL.

THE GLOWING EYES.

THE FIERCE BEAK.

AND THAT'S THE TRUTH ABOUT OWLS.

Whooo Knew?

This is my territory, and I don't share.
With people taking up more land for housing, farming, and industry, there's less room for owls. Please do us a favor and leave some old trees behind. We're some of the best all-natural "pest control" around.

25

HELPING OWLS

You can help owls and other wildlife by letting nature be wild. Avoid using chemicals that kill plants, insects, and rodents. As birds of prey, owls are at the top of the food chain. Owls might not eat poison, but if the animals they hunt do (or the prey eats plants that have been poisoned), the owl gets sick, too.

Some people help owls by providing an owl nesting box far from highways and away from land where chemicals are used. Be sure to learn more about owls native to your area before trying to attract an owl to your property. If you do hang a nesting box, research the size needed and add some pine needles or dried leaves to it. Most owls are highly territorial and guard against any potential food rivals or predators—including humans. So, keep a safe distance.

Anatomy of an Owl

ear tufts Ear tufts provide camouflage since they can look like branches. Owls move their ear tufts to communicate and show their moods. They do not help an owl to hear.

facial disks The feathers forming saucer-like circles around the owls' eyes work like satellite dishes. They capture and direct sounds to the ears on the sides of the head.

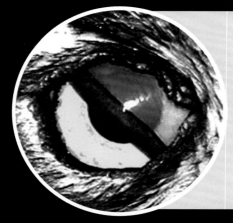

eyes Since owls see with both eyes at the same time (called binocular vision), they have the great depth perception needed to target prey. Each eye has a third, clear eyelid called the nictitating membrane.

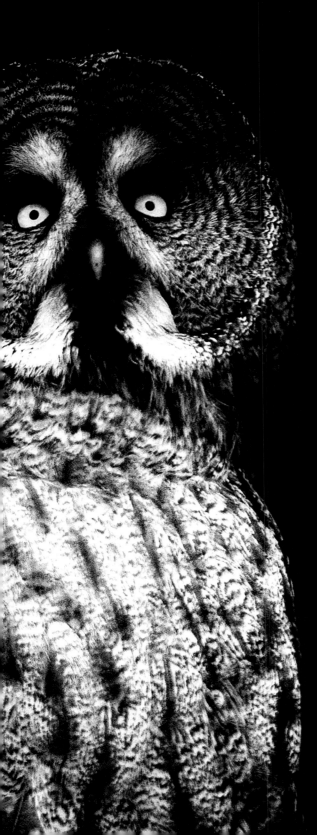

ears The ear openings hide below feathers on the side of the owl's head. Owls have the largest ear opening of any bird. One ear is often higher than the other.

feathers The markings on the owl's feathers camouflage the body. The wing feathers' edges are serrated, which enables the owl to fly silently. Feathers even cover and protect the owl's feet.

talons The needle-sharp talons have two forward-facing and two backward-facing toes. This arrangement allows the owl to grab and lock onto its prey.

WHAT'S FOR DINNER?

You can learn about an owl's meal by carefully dissecting—or examining—an owl pellet. What animals did the owl eat? How many?

You'll Need:

- paper plate (or other disposable work surface)
- tools like toothpicks, wooden probes, or wooden skewers
- owl pellet bone chart
- sterilized owl pellet
- disposable gloves and face masks
- antiseptic wipes

What to Do:

❶ Carefully open the aluminum foil wrapper around the pellet. Place the owl pellet on the paper plate.

❷ Using the tools, gently open the owl pellet and separate the bones from the fur or feathers.

❸ Clean the bones.

❹ Using the bone chart, try to identify the skulls inside the pellet. You might even be able to reconstruct the skeletons.

Note: Commercial owl pellets are sterilized and wrapped in aluminum foil prior to sale at some wildlife rehabilitation centers and online at science supply stores. If you collect owl pellets on your own, wrap them individually in aluminum foil and then bake at 250°F (121°C) for four hours to sterilize them. Let them cool before dissecting.

BONE CHART (VOLE)

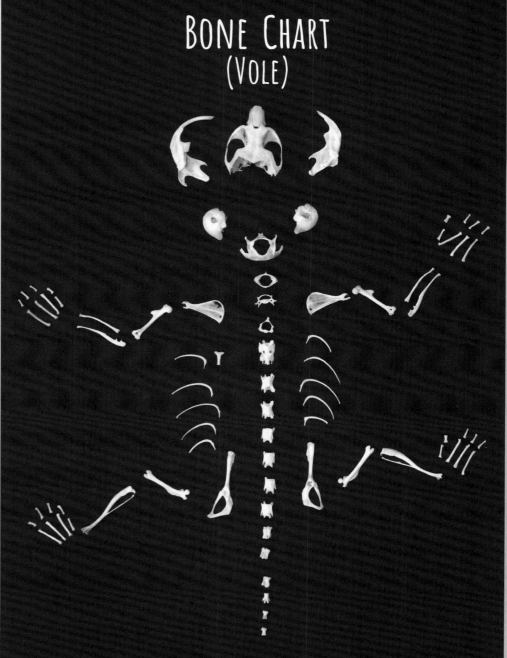

GLOSSARY

camouflage: the natural coloring of an animal that makes it hard to be seen in its surroundings

down: the soft, often fluffy, feathers of a bird

nocturnal: active at night

perch: a high place to sit and rest

predator: an animal that hunts other animals

prey: the animal hunted by other animals for food

vertebrae: the bones making up the backbone or spine

Some Helpful Websites

www.audubon.org

www.birdsoftheworld.org

www.explore.org

www.owling.com

www.owlpages.com

www.owlresearchinstitute.org

www.theowlstrust.org

ANNETTE WHIPPLE

loves to learn about the world around her through hands-on research. That's how she met Quincy, a Eurasian Eagle Owl. When Annette's not reading or writing, you might find her snacking on warm chocolate chip cookies with her family in Pennsylvania.

32